Mission, Vision & Values

Resource Tool Kit

Mark Villareal

People, Strategy, Execution

ISBN: 978-0-692-94960-3

ACKNOWLEDGEMENT

Having been in business for over 35-years, I have seen businesses succeed and fail. The most frustrating circumstance is where businesses fail due to a lack of having built their business on the foundation of proper Mission, Vision and Values. In addition, some businesses that may appear to have some success, may not be obtaining their full potential through the same circumstance. In my workshops, consulting and speeches, I demonstrate how the lack of this very foundation can create failure that we believe are derived from other situations. In my speech about planning, we define that many organizations are in a constant state of planning due to the lack of goal achievement. The failure has them searching for answers and blaming the goal, as being the problem. They terminate employees for lack of goal achievement and make adjustments to management and teams. Yet, they fail to determine that the problem is foundational and that it starts with culture. Culture is built with the creation of the right values and principles, driven throughout the organization and lived daily. Many organizations treat values and principles as a list on a wall, and may have committed the cardinal sin of sacrificing a value or principle for short term gain. When witnessed, employees then quickly follow the leader and understand that the values and principles are not of significant meaning to leadership.

However, with the right values and principles, an organization can then build a proper Mission and Vision Statement that adheres to the adopted values and principles. Mission is external, which means it defines why the company exists and the organizations purpose. Vision is internal to internal customers, the employees and shareholders of the organization. This should define the companies 3 to 5 year internal vision. This should include a BHAG; Big, Hairy, and Audacious Goal. It allows the organization to set their sights on growth, acquisitions, market domination and goal achievement. When each are built properly, adopted, and driven throughout an organization, the culture is driven and lived strong throughout. The values and principles act as a foundational guide that gives direction. The Mission then leads the way pulling the organization while the Vision pushes. When every decision adheres to the Mission, Vision, and the Values the organization is transparent, and each employee has clarity of their purpose and goal. The organization becomes a great place to work, where future employees seek to join the team. This is why I am so passionate on establishing Mission, Vision, and Values.

CONTENTS

BUILDING YOUR MISSION, VISION, AND VALUES RESOURCE TOOL KIT

The Mission, Vision and Values of an organization are of vital importance, as they are truly the lifeblood. However, many businesses fail to understand their importance and struggle within their organizations direction and execution yet, never realizing the connection. Strong organizations understand the importance of establishing proper Mission, Vision, and Values that are the foundation of the organization and by being the foundation, every decision, strategic plan, initiative, employee new hire, job description, manager accountability plans, and even termination must point back and adhere to the organizations Mission, Vision, and Values.

As business and industries change or adapt, the Mission, Vision, and Values may need to also evolve through evaluation and assessment. The process and its execution is also of extreme importance on defining the Mission, Vision, and Values of an organization. A process that includes the participation of leadership, employees, and advisors is recommended for inclusive feedback that when executed correctly, creates buy-in and accountability. Single owners or small businesses can utilize advisors from peer groups, and other trusted business owners to assist in building the Mission, Vision, and Values.

EXERCISE #1—VALUES & PRINCIPLES

PROBLEM: The problem that exists in many organizations today is that the leader, or leaders, do not take the time to establish a set of values that define the organization. This can be for several reasons. Perhaps the business was started by one person and they did not believe there was a need to execute a process of defining a set of core values. Many times a leader may believe values are common sense and automatic and that others will adhere to standard practices that match common sense. Other times a leader may believe it is best to wait on defining the values of an organization as they believe it is best to let the business grow, and by waiting to see how the business grows the values will help present themselves. Each of these have their faults when executed and can cause the business detrimental harm which cost money, time and progress. It may even cost the organization their employees and customers.

Values, when defined, give the organization a direction to build everything else upon. They can be re-evaluated as the company grows and the industry changes. By having no set values defined, there is no guidance in decision-making. This starts with job descriptions, the type of employee the organization would like to attract, to the products and services a business sells, and to how they sell and attract customers. No guidelines or direction creates confusion, which then creates bad decisions, or paralysis sets in, with the lack of decisions being made.

VALUES & PRINCIPLES: Values and principles are two different, yet similar items. Values can be defined as the following. "A list of adoptive beliefs of standards or behaviors." These can be defined as ethics, honesty, integrity, respect, morals, initiative, and much more. When values are adhered to, adopted and followed they become a principle, which means they are a habit and have become automatic. In my book "Leadership Lessons From Mom", I quote where my mother would teach me that values are what you live by and principles are what you stand on. It was important to my mother that I learned that my values had to be lived daily for my principles to become a habit that made them automatic. So if I claim a principle of honesty, and someone dropped money without knowing they dropped it, my principle would automatically and without hesitation let that person know. Because it is automatic my decision-making process did not have to contemplate to not inform the person that they dropped the money. A principle actually becomes a rule of law. If we are truly a believer in a principle, we hold ourselves accountable to this rule of law. For the purpose of this resource tool kit, we define both values and principles because some organizations may utilize them differently, yet effectively. So let's explore.

When an organization defines their values and adopt them, they will demonstrate that these values are the foundation of their identity. Values define what the company stands for internally and externally, and they define what the company embodies. Finally, their values will also define what their product or services contribute to the world. Organizations may list their values or define their values in value statements that places their values into an action statement.

Other organizations define principles, taking their values to the next level. They too can be defined in an action statement and listed as guiding principles. The organization will demonstrate their importance to their employees by not only educating everyone with whom they employ, but also their customers. They will display their values and principles and market them as competitive differentiators. The more people they educate, the more accountable they become.

This Resource Tool Kit defines a process for creating your organizations values and principles. The kit will explain and provide the education process, adoption process, and the evaluation and assessment process. The kit will also provide items of execution attached to the roll out of the values and principles for long term success.

The proper process on Mission, Vision and Values is to build the values first. This provides the foundation of every decision the organization will make, the employees they hire, and the culture they build. The Resource Tool Kit is built in a recommended order and process of execution. However, organizations have several moving parts, and the order and process can be altered to work within that organizations environment. We state with caution that any alteration still takes into account the full execution of the process.

BUILDING THE VALUES & PRINCIPLES

The rollout of building the values and principles of the organization are important. This is for several reasons:

1. As a leader, you want to demonstrate and explain the importance of establishing the organizations values and principles.

2. As a leader, you want to educate everyone on why this process is important, what it means to you and the organization, and how the values and principles will be the foundation of the culture of the organization and every decision.

3. This is the time to explain the process, timelines and measurements. It is important to explain participation, accountability, and why inclusiveness is important.

4. Finally, every leader shares a vision. Share a vision of how you desire the process to work. How you expect, and appreciate, feedback for the betterment of the organization.

PRE-ROLLOUT DETERMINATIONS:

1. Leadership team involvement—It is important to have the leadership team defined so they will be notified on their involvement. The team can and should assist in cheerleading the process and accounting for their team's participation.

2. If you are an organization where you are the only person, or have few employees, designate other business leaders whose opinions you value. Ask them to participate. Educate them on the process.

3. Define group meetings that will be necessary. This is determined by the size of an organization and how many locations if there is more than one. Technology has allowed for internet-connected meetings to be scheduled, but in-person meetings, when possible, still add value to demonstrate the importance of the program.

4. Define how you will communicate. Things to be considered are:

A) Spokesman—Usually the top leader, but this can be delegated.

B) Email template communication announcing the program.

C) Email template communication announcing the meeting and the process.

D) Survey & Questionnaire process: Paper or through Electronic Survey Process (Survey Monkey)

E) How timeline, deadlines, and past due notifications will be communicated.

F) How initial rollout meeting will be conducted.

G) How selection of the values and principles will be conducted and communicated.

H) How meeting for rollout of values and principles will be conducted.

I) Timeline for each.

PRE-ROLLOUT LEADERSHIP INITIAL MEETING:

1. Email Leadership Team a schedule request for the meeting to define the organizations values.

2. Email leadership survey requesting feedback and insight. (Sample enclosed)

3. Send an attached document explaining what values and principles are with the outlining of some basic standard values. (Sample enclosed)

4. If this is a re-assessment of new values or principles for the organization, then have each member bring a copy of the current values or principles and ask them to be prepared to speak to any they believe are <u>not being executed and why, and if they need to be changed, altered or re-purposed for another rollout</u>.

5. Encourage each member to look at other organizations values and principles, how that organization may live and demonstrate them, and what they like or dislike about them.

6. Encourage employees to be open and honest, as well as respectful of others.

INITIAL MEETING—LEADERSHIP:

1. Have a whiteboard ready or large wall-sized Post It Notes that can hang on a wall.

2. If you have current values or principles, and this is a re-assessment, then have a large list of current values or principles.

3. Have each leader list values they believe should be adopted on whiteboard or large wall-sized Post It Notes.

4. Have each member explain why they believe in the values they listed. Listen for the passion. Ask how they will be utilized in the business.

5. Review survey results taken from leadership, note any items not brought forth yet.

6. Allow debate, but must be respectful.

7. Define some core values, does not have to be total agreement as the next stage of the process will debate, might eliminate, or add more.

INITIAL EMPLOYEE MEETING:

1. Send out, via email, initial survey asking for feedback and insight. Allow 24 to 48 hours for response.

2. After return of initial survey, send out questionnaire to employees with the list of values leadership team recommended. Explain that these values are a starting point and you are asking for feedback, pushback, and any recommended additions.

3. Explain that with any recommended additions, the request that the submitting employee define with passion why the addition, or additions, should be added, how they should be utilized in the business, and how the business will benefit.

4. Give a deadline for survey return.

5. Work with leadership on outstanding surveys and questionnaires.

6. Gather together all surveys and questionnaires. Have an assigned person list results of each, survey and questionnaire, in a rollup document. Note: do not list employee names as this is supposed to be anonymous.

7. Set follow-up leadership meeting.

FOLLOW-UP LEADERSHIP MEETING:

1. Have notes available from initial meeting, have on display if possible.

2. Ask for insight prior to reviewing employee survey feedback from leadership. What interaction is the leadership team seeing with the staff? Note the discussions on involvement or lack of involvement. Be encouraging and demonstrate concern if necessary.

3. Have the assigned person who listed the results of survey in a rollup document present. Have presentation on overhead if possible, if not have in individual handouts.

4. Allow for leadership to ask for any clarification. Debate any feedback and discuss any new suggestions.

5. Have the assigned person who listed the results of questionnaire in a rollup document present. Have presentation on overhead if possible, if not have in individual handouts.

6. Allow for leadership to ask for any clarification. Debate any feedback and discuss any new suggestions.

7. Define your set values. Should be a minimum of five but can be more if each are unique and bring additional insight. Important: Leadership is a molder of consensus not a builder of consensus. This means that the final determinations are made by the leader and the leadership team. The purpose of the exercise is to demonstrate openly and effectively that the process is inclusive, feedback is appreciated, and all things were taken into account.

8. Review with leadership team and ask openly:

   A) Do the values define your organization?

   B) Will the values help establish a strong culture?

   C) Do the values demonstrate how you want to be represented to your external customer?

   D) Do the values hold you accountable?

   E) Can you live, stand, and not stray from the values, even through difficult times?

   F) Do the values allow for an evolving and changing industry and encourage and support innovation?

   G) Can you see the team rally around the values?

9. After review, then officially adopt the values.

10. Define how you want the values listed. The options are:

    A) Leave as single words as a value. Examples are: Integrity, Trust, Celebrate, Fun, Ethics, etc.

    B) Create value statements. Value statements are an effective way to demonstrate the values in action. They are also an effective way to teach memorization by individual employees. Many organizations, when possible, take the first letter of each value statement to spell a word which helps in memorization. Teach the word, and everyone then knows each first letter of the beginning of each Value Statement. There is an example of Mr. V. Consulting Value Statements where the first letter of each Value Statement spells HITREACT. The employees learn to memorize HITREACT and they then know the first letter of each Value Statement and it is a step forward in memorizing each statement.

C) Establish Guiding Principles: Values can be utilized to define Guiding Principles. Principles are automatic and allows the organization to demonstrate what they stand for. A guiding principle is the result of a value in action. Some Guiding Principle examples are:

1) To always do the next right thing. (Integrity in action)

2) We choose to be positive. (Fun in action)

3) We are determined to complete all plans to fruition. (Achievement in action)

11. Define a communication plan. A communication plan includes:

A) Timeline of dates and times of communications.

B) How it will be communicated. (Live meeting, online meeting, etc.)

C) Who will be presenting.

D) Any marketing flyers. (Highly recommended)

E) Materials that add to the marketing role out. Balloons, food, drinks.

F) Website presence and how to address it with customers.

G) Contest for demonstrating the values.

H) Contest for memorizing the values.

I) Expectations and accountability.

J) Any new email signature guidelines that include values (Not always recommended. Limited space.)

K) Any other marketing materials (Stress balls, coasters, pencils, pens.)

COMPANY ROLL OUT OF VALUES MEETING:

1. Be prepared to make it an exciting event. Be upbeat and add some fun and humor into the presentation.

2. Give a quick review on how the process worked and thank everyone for their participation.

3. Once again explain the importance of the values and how they are the foundation for the culture of the organization and every decision will be built upon this foundation.

4. Explain the expectations of everyone learning the values through memorization, and holding each other accountable.

5. Pass out the marketing flyer on the values and review. Explain each value. Give real world examples that employees can relate to.

6. Describe the contest on people living the values, rewards available, and timelines.

7. Review the expectation once again of living the values.

8. Define, if necessary, any additional marketing of the values, email signature lines, website visibility, and swag materials.

FOLLOWING DAYS AND WEEKS:

The most effective ways to follow-up is for you, as the leaders, to demonstrate the values or principles and their importance. Any meetings, whether live, over the phone, or via internet, open each meeting by randomly quizzing individuals on the values or principles. Ask for examples of employees living the values or principles. Be fun, but also hold individuals accountable. Be encouraging to those that struggle when asked to recite a value or principle, and express the importance again. Your consistency on this process is what will demonstrate to others the importance. Your example will encourage other leaders to do the same, and eventually it will spread throughout the business.

Make sure the contest associated with the values or principles are followed-up on and that all timelines are met. It is important to ensure that the values or principles get integrated into the culture of the organization. Missing deadlines for contests is a killer of culture. When contest winners achieve, reward them, announce it with company communication methods. This communication can be live during a meeting, via email, announced on external website, and internal intranets, etc. Make the prizes unique and even add in a twist, such as unique business cards for the winners. Be creative.

EVALUATION AND ASSESSMENT:

Values and principles can last for a long time for an organization. Usually because values and principles are foundational. However, sometimes because of industry changes, acquisitions, new or reduced products and services, and growth in employees or locations, you may determine that it is desirable to evaluate and assess your current values or principles. The process is the same that is described in this document. First recommendation is to review with the leadership team if the values or principles have gone stale due to leadership not keeping them alive. This is an honest question and it is not uncommon for leaders to lose sight of the importance on keeping values or principles in the forefront. This is the best starting point to assess before engaging in the process. Many times, when going through an evaluation process, most organizations may just find a need to add a new value or principle while keeping the others, or possibly only changing one or two to match the current situation.

MR. V. CONSULTING SERVICES VALUE STATEMENTS

Humility: To engage with any person, team or organization with no preconceived notions or opinions that allow us to determine the details of the current landscape.

Integrity: To perform to our fullest capabilities in solution development and understanding our expertise.

Trust: To earn the trust of our clients to consult professionally and confront issues for the benefit of both parties.

Respect: To conduct ourselves professionally and appropriately and to treat everyone as a ten.

Ethics: To always do the next right thing.

Achievement: To understand and define the needs of our clients and determine a path for success.

Celebrate: To enjoy success of others and celebrate milestones.

Train: To pass on knowledge with passion.

EMAIL TEMPLATES

Announcing the decision and process for building the organizations Values & Principles:

Subject: Values & Principles

To all employees,

All, we as an organization, have decided and defined a process in which we will create and define our organizations values and principles. Because each of you are a valued part of our business, we need your participation, insight and feedback, so that we can construct values and principles that we all believe and live each day, and demonstrate who we are as an organization. Values and principles help define our very culture as an organization and should encompass our beliefs that we exhibit to both our internal and external customer. The seriousness of defining values and principles that match our organization is important as they will give us a direction in which to build our Mission Statement, and Vision Statement. Our values and principles will guide us daily. Our Mission Statement will lead us and our Vision Statement will push us all in the same direction. Great companies build and live their Mission, Vision and Values. Our values will build the foundation of every decision we make as an organization, starting with the Mission and Vision that then builds our strategic plans, initiatives, accountability plans, roadmaps, development plans, job descriptions, employee hiring and more. Let's make the process fun and exciting. You will be asked to participate in surveys and feedback and your response and timeliness will be appreciated.

Meeting: (Announce place, time, and method of meeting)

Sincerely,

Management

Email announcing the Values & Principles Survey

Subject: Values & Principles Survey

To all employees,

As we move forward with the process of defining and adopting our organizations values and principles, please take a moment and answer the questions on the attached survey. There is an additional section for further comments and feedback. Your information will remain confidential. Timeliness is very important, and we desire and would like to achieve 100% participation. If you have any questions please contact your supervisor or HR. (If survey is online simply supply the link or directions and adjust email)

Deadline: (Insert date)

Sincerely,

Management

Email announcing the Values & Principles Questionnaire

Subject: Values & Principles Questionnaire

To all employees,

As we move forward with the process of defining and adopting our organizations values and principles, please take a moment and review the list of values that your leadership team defined as ones to consider for possible adoption. Please make a comment after each value if you feel strongly in the values adoption, not strongly, or non-committal. There is an additional section for further comments and feedback. Please list any extra values you deem of value in the additional comments section. Your information will remain confidential. Timeliness is very important, and we desire and would like to achieve 100% participation. If you have any questions please contact your supervisor or HR. (If questionnaire is online simply supply the link or directions and adjust email)

Deadline: (Insert date)

Sincerely,

Management

Announcing the rollout of the values & principles. (After rollout meeting)

Subject: Values & Principles Rollout Meeting!

To all employees,

It is with great excitement that we announce we have achieved our goal on building our organizations values and principles. Our values and principles will be the very definition on who we are as an organization and the very foundation of every decision moving forward. We desire 100% participation to this important rollout meeting. We ask for your promptness and awareness.

Meeting date: (List date, time, duration and method of meeting)

Sincerely,

Management

Announcing the organizations values & principles

Subject: Our Values & Principles (can be altered based upon what you decided to build, value statements, guiding principles, or just a list of values.)

To all employees,

Our process is complete and I wish to thank everyone in our organization for their participation. To have an organization that we can be proud of means having an organization that lives and demonstrates the values and principles that we defined as a team and adopted. Let's show each other, our teams, our customers, and even our future employees that we are an organization that others want to be associated with. Below is a list of our values and principles. (List what you defined. Alter email as needed.)

Please post your marketing brochure on our values and principles prominently in your work area.

Sincerely,

Management

Email announcing importance of memorizing the values or principles

Subject: Importance of knowing our values (alter as needed based upon values or principles)

To all employees,

Our organization has completed an important task in defining our values. Your participation, providing feedback and insight, added invaluable contributions in their completion. With their completion we, as an organization, must hold ourselves accountable by living them each day. Our marketing will display them to our customers in our materials and website presence. I implore each of us to commit them to memory and celebrate them in action. We will have continual contests, rewards, and accountability to enhance our learning.

Sincerely,

Management

Email, sent at random times, announcing someone who has demonstrated the values.

Subject: Awesome display of our values (alter as needed)

To all employees,

I am so excited to see our values being demonstrated. *First Name Last Name* demonstrated our value of responsibility by recognizing an area where we did not fully complete a project for a client, although we believed we did. Certainly, we wish to avoid scenarios like this. However, because we are responsible to our customers, *First Name Last Name* took initiative and personal accountability and contacted the client, spoke honestly and professionally, and let them know we would follow through with satisfactory completion. The client understood, and appreciated our honesty and concern. This is living our values and I wanted to share with our entire staff. My personal thanks to *First Name Last Name*.

Sincerely,

Management

VALUES & PRINCIPLES (ATTACHMENT)

Our organization values your employment and daily contribution. It is with this appreciation that we are requesting your participation in the development of our organizations values and principles. Leadership will communicate the process for the development as well as your assignment and timelines. Below are brief definitions of values, principles and the value statements and principle statements.

VALUES: Values are a set of beliefs and standards. Values for an organization are important as they set the foundation of what that organization will demonstrate based upon those beliefs and standards.

EXAMPLES OF VALUES:

Integrity	Honesty	Trust	Ethics	Respect
Responsibility	Accountability	Initiative	Celebrate	Fun
Achievement	Joy	Boldness	Determination	Presistence

VALUE STATEMENTS: Value Statements take a value and turn it into a value statement, which places it in action. This is an effective way to gain an understanding of the value and it's positioning within an organization. A value statement can define for your customers a demonstration of your organizations standards and beliefs. It also can be a market differentiator between you and your competitors.

EXAMPLES OF VALUE STATEMENTS:

Take initiative and expect accountability.

Respect each other and treat others like you would like to be treated.

Put ethics first in every decision.

Celebrate success and achievement.

PRINCIPLES AND PRINCIPLE STATEMENTS: When values are adopted and adhered to they become a principle, which means they become a habit and are automatic. When something is a principle within an individual the value is established within their mindset. This is why, at times, organizations define their values and develop guiding principles, which, like a value statement, are placed into action in a statement. A guiding principle statement is the result of the action of a value.

EXAMPLES OF PRINCIPLE STATEMENTS:

1) To always do the next right thing. **(Integrity in action)**

2) We choose to be positive. **(Fun in action)**

3) We are determined to complete all plans to fruition. **(Achievement in action)**

SURVEY—VALUES & PRINCIPLES

Please answer the questions on this survey. Use all the space necessary as your feedback is greatly appreciated. Please be professional, yet forthright. Your comments and answers will be confidential.

1. What are the current listed values of our organization, if any?

_____

_____

_____

_____

_____

2. Through example, what values and/or principles does our organization exhibit?

_____

_____

_____

_____

_____

3. Are there values that our organization lacks? Be specific and give examples when possible.

_____

_____

_____

_____

_____

4. What are some of your personal values and/or principles that you would like to share, and why are they important?

_____

_____

_____

_____

_____

5. Are there values and principles that you believe would be of value to our organization and why?

_____

_____

_____

_____

_____

6. Why are values and principles important in an organization in regards to their internal customers, the employees?

_____

_____

_____

_____

_____

7. Why are values and principles important in an organization in regards to their external customers?

_____

_____

_____

_____

_____

8. What companies, other than ours, do you believe effectively demonstrate strong values and principles and why?

_____

_____

_____

_____

_____

9. What are some of the best examples that other organizations display and exhibit their values and principles?

_____

_____

_____

_____

_____

_____

10. Please rank the following values on a scale of 1 through 17

     A) Trust _____

     B) Integrity _____

     C) Honesty _____

     D) Ethics _____

     E) Respect _____

     F) Initiative _____

     G) Fun _____

     H) Celebration _____

     I) Achievement _____

     J) Accountability _____

     K) Knowledge _____

     L) Recognition _____

     M) Transparency _____

     N) Excellence _____

     O) Impact _____

     P) Joy _____

     Q) Courage _____

11. Please provide your perception on the contribution and impact that this organization makes to the community or should make?

_____

_____

_____

_____

_____

12. Please provide any additional feedback?

_____

_____

_____

_____

_____

_____

_____

_____

_____

VALUES QUESTIONNAIRE

In an effort to streamline and jump start the process on our organizations development of our values and principles, our leadership team met and listed values that they believe should be considered for adoption. This does not preclude any additional values from being added, nor does it define that the values listed must make it to the final list. Consider the value list as a starting point to assist in helping our team in the next stage of defining our organizations values.

Below is a list of each value the leadership team defined. Please select for each value a choice for:

Agree Strongly ( )   Somewhat Agree ( )   or   Non-Committal ( )

Value 1:	Agree Strongly ( )	Somewhat Agree ( )	Non-Committal ( )
Value 2:	Agree Strongly ( )	Somewhat Agree ( )	Non-Committal ( )
Value 3:	Agree Strongly ( )	Somewhat Agree ( )	Non-Committal ( )
Value 4:	Agree Strongly ( )	Somewhat Agree ( )	Non-Committal ( )
Value 5:	Agree Strongly ( )	Somewhat Agree ( )	Non-Committal ( )
Value 6:	Agree Strongly ( )	Somewhat Agree ( )	Non-Committal ( )
Value 7:	Agree Strongly ( )	Somewhat Agree ( )	Non-Committal ( )
Value 8:	Agree Strongly ( )	Somewhat Agree ( )	Non-Committal ( )
Value 9:	Agree Strongly ( )	Somewhat Agree ( )	Non-Committal ( )
Value 10:	Agree Strongly ( )	Somewhat Agree ( )	Non-Committal ( )

Additional Comments and Feedback:

_____

_____

_____

_____

_____

_____

_____

_____

_____

_____

_____

_____

_____

_____

_____

_____

EXERCISE #2—MISSION STATEMENT:

PROBLEM: As mentioned, in regards to values and principles, many companies and organizations do not understand the importance of a Mission Statement. Some may believe that it is not important to have a Mission Statement when starting their business. They believe that as the organization grows that at some later point a Mission Statement can then be defined. Sole proprietorships and small businesses may not see a need of a Mission Statement nor want to devote the proper time and research to develop one. Some leaders may believe they are just as effective of creating a Mission Statement from crafty words or catchy phrases, or they just create one on their own with little or no consideration and insight from advisors or employees.

WHY IS THIS A PROBLEM? This can be problematic due to the very nature of what a Mission Statement is supposed to help effect within the organization. With this lack of understanding one may not realize the power of an effective Mission Statement. A proper Mission Statement is built on the foundation of the organizations values and principles. If built correctly, the values and principles act as a guide of direction to ensure that the Mission, Vision, and every decision adheres to the values and the principles. When aligned, a Mission Statement then gives clear and transparent direction for the organization that every employee understands and is held accountable to the Mission. With the lack of a Mission Statement, employees lack the clarity and transparency of a purpose and a defined direction. It opens up opportunities of less accountability and buy-in by the employee staff. With the lack of a Mission Statement, employees perform the job description duties at best, with limited initiative.

A Mission Statement gives an organization their purpose, which defines why they exist. When created and adopted correctly, a Mission Statement can clarify to customers why you are different than your competitors and why your organization is a benefit to theirs. I recall a story that occurred in the past of when I was a General Manager of a sales organization. I and one of our sales personnel went on a sales meeting to a client's location. The department head of one of the customers' business units introduced themselves and their first question directed at us was, "What is your organizations Mission Statement?" The sales person I was with struggled to answer. Fortunately, I was able to provide the answer and include how our Mission Statement would benefit them. That is the strength of a Mission Statement, because it is your purpose for existence, and you can define to a customer how your purpose benefits them. Understanding your Mission and your customer are equally important and has power when tied together. In addition, by being asked this question, it immediately brought awareness that culture was important to the organization we were meeting with, as well as within their leadership. The assumption was correct, as the company was Rackspace, where everyone in the organization knows and lives their Mission daily. Their Mission Statement is driven top down and bottom up.

Equally as important, a Mission Statement defines for your external customer why you exist and your purpose. It also defines this to your internal customer, your employees. This is important because when employees understand your Mission Statement, they can then align with the Mission. This allows you to give insight and guidance on how to grow and take initiative. When employees understand how they can develop professionally while being in alignment with executing your Mission, they and your organization benefit. Imagine an employee asking, understanding and executing their job knowledge and development around your Mission. As they advance, others would take the initiative for their own growth and advancement. The Mission would advance in execution, which then grows your organization.

Now understanding that a Mission Statement is external, which means it is client facing, it also by definition is not something that should be a secret. We teach and consult with organizations that their Mission Statement should be listed on their website, in email signatures, on business cards, around reception areas and displayed throughout the organization. The Mission Statement should serve as a constant reminder and motivation. But by also proudly displaying your organizations Mission Statement, it becomes an accountability piece. As a leader leads by example they also demonstrate there is no fear in having your customers and all staff hold the business accountable.

MISSION VERSUS VISION:

There are several different beliefs and methods in regards to Mission Statements and Vision Statements. A Mission Statement, as mentioned, is your purpose and reason for existence. It is external for your customers to see and understand, but it also works internally for your employees to align with. A Vision Statement is internal-facing, and based upon the stage of the organization, is usually a 3 to 5 year vision. When defining a Vision, market and competitive analysis allow the organization to define a BHAG, Big Hairy Audacious Goal, which should be larger than life. It can include what it would look like to dominate your market, expand services and products, and perhaps acquire other businesses. This is generally why a Vision Statement is internal, as it is the driving force for your leaders and all employees. It might appear arrogant to customers, but ambitious to your employees.

The proper process, as mentioned, is to have built your organizations values first, as this will allow you to align your Mission Statement to your values and principles. It also serves as a reminder that every decision must align to the values and principles too.

BUILDING THE MISSION STATEMENT

The rollout of building the Mission Statement of the organization is important. This is for several reasons:

1. As a leader, you want to demonstrate and explain the importance of establishing the organizations Mission Statement.

2. As a leader, you want to educate everyone why this process is important, and what a proper Mission Statement defines for you and the organization. It is important to demonstrate how the Mission Statement will be built on the foundation of the culture of the organization and every decision will flow back through the Mission to the organizations values and principles.

3. This is the time to explain the process, timelines and measurements. It is important to explain participation, accountability, and why inclusiveness is important.

4. Finally, every leader shares a vision. Share a vision of how you desire the process to work. Communicate how you expect and appreciate feedback for the betterment of the organization.

PRE-ROLLOUT DETERMINATIONS:

1. Leadership team involvement—It is important to have the leadership team defined so that they will be notified on their involvement. The team can and should assist in cheerleading the process and accounting for their team's participation.

2. If you are an organization where you are the only person, or with a small staff, define other business leaders whose opinions you value. Ask them to participate. Educate them on the process.

3. Define group meetings that will be necessary. This is determined by the size of an organization and how many locations, if more than one. Technology has allowed for internet connected meetings to be scheduled, however, in-person meetings, when possible, still add value to demonstrate the importance of the program.

4. Define how you will communicate. Things to be considered are:

A) Spokesman—Usually top leader, however, this can be delegated.

B) Email template communication announcing the program.

C) Email template communication announcing the meeting and the process.

D) Survey process: Paper or through Electronic Survey Process (Survey Monkey)

E) How timeline, deadlines, and past due notifications will be communicated.

F) How initial rollout meeting will be conducted.

G) How the building of the Mission Statement will be conducted and communicated.

H) How meeting for rollout of the Mission Statement will be conducted.

I) Timeline for the process.

PRE-ROLLOUT LEADERSHIP INITIAL MEETING:

1. Email Leadership Team of Meeting to define the organizations Mission Statement.

2. Send attached document explaining what a Mission Statement is.

3. If this is a re-assessment of a new Mission Statement for the organization, then have each member bring a copy of current existing Mission Statement and ask them to be prepared to speak to if they believe current one is not being executed and why, and if it needs to be changed, altered or re-purposed for another rollout.

4. Encourage each member to look at other organizations Mission Statement. Challenge them to define how that organization lives and demonstrates their Mission, and what they like or dislike about those examples.

5. Encourage openness and honesty, and respectfulness of others.

INITIAL MEETING—LEADERSHIP:

1. Have whiteboard ready or large wall-sized Post It Notes for hanging on wall.

2. If you have a current Mission Statement, or if this is a re-assessment, then have a list with the current Mission Statement listed.

3. Have each leader list considerations for a Mission, or their perception of the organizations purpose. List these on whiteboard or large wall-sized Post It Notes.

4. Have each member explain why they believe in the purpose or Mission they listed. Listen for the passion. Ask how they will be utilized in the business.

5. Allow for respectful debate.

6. Define some good examples of a Mission or purpose for the organizations existence. There does not have to be total agreement as the next stage of the process will debate, and might eliminate, or add more.

INITIAL EMPLOYEE MEETING:

1. Based on size, send out survey with list of each purpose and Mission leadership defined.

2. Explain that these Mission ideas are a starting point and you are asking for feedback, pushback, and any recommended additions.

3. Explain that with any recommended additions, a request that the submitting employee define with passion why the addition, or additions, should be added, how they should be utilized in the business, and how the business will benefit.

4. Give a deadline for survey return.

5. Work with leadership on outstanding surveys.

6. Gather together all surveys. Have someone assigned that lists results in a rollup document. Note: do not list employee names as this is supposed to be anonymous.

7. Set follow-up leadership meeting.

FOLLOW-UP LEADERSHIP MEETING:

1. Have notes available from initial meeting, have on display if possible.

2. Ask for insight prior to reviewing employee survey feedback from leadership. What interaction is the leadership team seeing with the staff? Note the discussions on involvement or lack of involvement. Be encouraging and demonstrate concern if necessary.

3. Have assigned person who listed the results in a rollup document present results. Have presentation on overhead if possible, if not have in individual handouts.

4. Allow for leadership to ask for any clarification. Debate any feedback and discuss any new suggestions.

5. Define your set Mission Statement moving forward. Important: Leadership is a molder of consensus not a builder of consensus. This means that the final determinations are made by the leader and the leadership team. The purpose of the exercise is to demonstrate openly and effectively that the process is inclusive, feedback is appreciated, and all things were taken into account.

6. Review with leadership team and ask openly:

A) Does the Mission Statement define your organizations purpose and reason for existence?

B) Will the Mission Statement add clarity and help establish a strong culture?

C) Does the Mission Statement represent how your organization should be viewed by your external customers?

D) Does the Mission Statement include accountability?

E) Can you live, stand, and not stray from the Mission Statement, even through difficult times?

F) Does the Mission Statement allow for an evolving and changing industry and encourage and support innovation?

G) Can you envision the team rallying around the Mission Statement?

E) Can you easily explain the benefits of the Mission Statement?

7. Final review, then adopt the Mission Statement.

8. Define how you want the Mission Statement listed. The options are:

A) On your customer-facing website where you list 5 to 7 benefits to clients.

B) Listed on a marketing piece for internal use to keep employees aware, also listing 5 to 7 benefits to clients.

C) Listed in email signatures of employees.

D) Some organizations might do a marketing piece announcing the organization has established and set a new Mission Statement. This can demonstrate your evolution.

9. Define a communication plan. A communication plan includes:

A) Timeline of dates and times of communications.

B) How it will be communicated. (Live meeting, online meeting, etc.)

C) Who will be presenting.

D) Any marketing flyers (Highly recommended)

E) Materials that add to the marketing rollout. (Balloons, food, drinks)

F) Website presence and recommendation on how to address it with customers.

G) Contest for demonstrating the Mission Statement.

H) Contest for memorizing the Mission Statement and benefits.

I) Expectations and accountability.

J) Any new email signature guidelines.

K) Any other marketing materials (Stress balls, coasters, pencils, pens)

COMPANY ROLLOUT OF MISSION STATEMENT MEETING:

1. Be prepared to make it an exciting event. Be upbeat and add some fun and humor into the presentation.

2. Give a quick review on how the process worked and thank everyone for their participation.

3. Once again explain the importance of the Mission Statement and how the Mission Statement is built on the foundation of the culture of the organization. Also that every decision will be built upon this foundation from the Mission Statement and Vision Statement, aligning with the organizations values and principles.

4. Explain the expectations of everyone learning the Mission Statement and benefits through memorization, as well as holding each other accountable.

5. Pass out the marketing flyer on the Mission Statement and review. Explain each benefit. Give real world examples that employees can relate to.

6. Describe the contest recognizing employees who demonstrate through action that they are living the Mission Statement. Describe the rewards available, and timelines.

7. Review the expectation and importance of living the Mission Statement.

8. Define, if necessary, any additional marketing of the Mission Statement, email signature lines, website visibility, and swag materials.

9. It is recommended that you rollout the Vision Statement at the same time as the Mission Statement.

FOLLOWING DAYS AND WEEKS:

The most effective ways to follow-up is for you, as the leaders, to demonstrate the Mission Statement and its importance. Any meetings, whether live, over the phone, or internet, open each meeting by randomly quizzing individuals on the Mission Statement. Ask for examples of employees living the Mission Statement. Be fun, but also hold individuals accountable. With individual employees that struggle, encourage them to learn and express again the importance. Your consistency on this process is what will demonstrate to others the importance. Your example will encourage other leaders to do the same, and eventually it will spread throughout the business.

Make sure any contest associated with the Mission Statement is followed up upon and that all timelines are met. It is important to ensure that the Mission Statement get integrated into the culture of the organization. Missing deadlines for contests is a killer of culture. When contest winners make achievements, reward results, and announce the achievement with communication. This communication can be live during a meeting, via email, announced on external website, and intranet sites, etc. Make the prizes unique and even add in a twist, such as a unique business card for the winners. Be creative.

EVALUATION AND ASSESSMENT:

A Mission Statement can last for a long time for an organization. Usually because the Mission Statement is from the foundational process that started with values and principles. However, sometimes because of industry changes, acquisitions, product and services additions or subtractions, and growth in employees or locations, you may determine that it is desirable to evaluate and re-assess your current Mission Statement. The process is the same that is described in this document. First recommendation is to review with the leadership team if the Mission Statement has gone stale due to leadership not keeping the Mission alive. This is an honest question and it is not uncommon for leaders to lose sight of the importance on keeping the Mission Statement in the forefront. This is the best starting point to re-assess before engaging in the process. Many times, when going through an evaluation process, most organizations may just find a need to add a new benefit while keeping the existing, or possibly only changing one or two benefits of the Mission statement to match the current landscape.

EXERCISE #3—VISION STATEMENT:

PROBLEM: As mentioned, in regards to values and principles, many companies and organizations do not understand the importance of a Vision Statement. Some may believe that it is not important to have a Vision Statement when they start their business. They believe that as the organization grows, that at some point a Vision Statement can then be defined. Sole proprietorships and small businesses may not see a need of a Vision Statement nor want to devote the proper time and research to develop one. Some leaders may believe they are just as effective of creating a Vision Statement from crafty words or catchy phrases, or they just create one on their own with little or no consideration and insight from advisors or employees.

WHY IS THIS A PROBLEM? This can be problematic due to the very nature of what a Vision Statement is supposed to help effect within the organization. With the lack of understanding a leader will fail to realize the power of an effective Vision Statement. A proper Mission Statement is built on the foundation of the organizations values and principles. If built correctly, the values and principles act as a guide of direction to ensure that the Mission, Vision, and every decision adheres to the values and the principles. When aligned, a Vision Statement gives clear and transparent direction for the organization that every employee understands and is held accountable to. With the lack of a Vision Statement, employees lack the clarity and transparency of an internal target and a defined direction that connects with the Mission Statement. It opens up opportunity of less accountability and buy-in by the employee staff. With the lack of a Vision Statement, employees perform the job description duties at best. Lack of a Vision Statement will also limit employee initiative.

A Vision Statement gives an organization their lofty goals and standards, which defines what they are attempting to achieve and strive for. When created and adopted correctly, a Vision Statement can clarify to your internal customers why goal achievement is so important, what are the overall expectations, and how achievement can benefit them. I recall a story that occurred in the past of when a leader of an organization desired to have enough innovation to create a new product each year that would assist in market domination. Yet, they did not communicate this desire. Because employees were not educated on this desire, they were not motivated to be innovative, take extra initiative, nor understand how they can help that organization achieve. Soon that employer would lose some employees to competitors and became frustrated as the very same employees would help the competitor grow because they were encouraged by an organization that established and communicated a vision of innovation, as well as rewarded initiative. That is the strength of a Vision Statement, because it is your organizations internal communication for achievement. It sets lofty goals and standards and identifies high expectations. Understanding your Vision empowers employees to take initiative, work on personal development, and contribute to growth and sustainability. In addition, your Vision Statement gives your Mission Statement the power to fuel its success. Great leaders share the Vision constantly, and establish milestones to demonstrate and measure if the Vision is being accomplished.

Employees that understand your Vision Statement can effectively align with both the Mission and Vision. This allows leadership to give insight and guidance on areas of development. When employees understand how they can develop professionally with alignment by executing your Mission and Vision, they and your organization benefit. Imagine an employee asking, understanding and executing their job knowledge and development around your Mission and Vision. As they advance, others would take the initiative for their own growth and advancement and the Vision would advance in achievement, which grows your organization and creates additional opportunity.

Unlike a Mission Statement that is external, which means it is client-facing, a Vision Statement is internal for employees, advisors, and investors. Your organizations Vision Statement, by being internal, should be displayed and communicated to your internal customer, your employees. The Vision Statement should serve as a constant reminder and motivation. Adding milestones and communicating milestone achievements from leadership adds to the motivation and builds a bridge for greater accountability. Leaders constantly share the Vision.

MISSION VERSUS VISION: (REPEAT)

There are several different beliefs and methods in regards to Mission Statements and Vision Statements. A Mission Statement, as mentioned, is your purpose and reason for existence. It is external for your customers to see and understand, but it also works internally for your employees to align with. A Vision Statement is internal-facing and, based upon the stage of the organization, is usually a 3 to 5 year vision. When defining a Vision, market and competitive analysis allow the organization to define a BHAG, Big Hairy Audacious Goal, which should be larger than life. It can include what it would look like to dominate your market, expand services and products, and perhaps acquire other businesses. This is generally why a Vision Statement is internal as it is the driving force for your leaders and all employees. It may appear arrogant to customers, but ambitious to your employees.

As mentioned, the proper process is to have built your organizations values first, as this will allow you to align your Mission Statement and Vision Statement to your values and principles. It also serves as a reminder that every decision must align to the values and principles.

BUILDING THE VISION STATEMENT

Note: The Vision Statement process should be executed in conjunction with the Mission Statement process. The meetings with leadership and employees should include both the content of the Mission Statement and Vision Statement exercises.

The rollout of building the Vison Statement of the organization is important. This is for several reasons:

1. As a leader, you want to demonstrate and explain the importance of establishing the organizations Vision Statement.

2. As a leader, you want to educate to everyone why this process is important and what a proper Vision Statement defines for you as well as the organization. It is important to demonstrate how the Vision Statement will be built on the foundation of the culture of the organization and every decision will flow back through the Vision to the organizations values and principles.

3. This is the time to explain the process, timelines and measurements. It is important to explain participation, accountability, and why inclusiveness is important.

4. Finally, every leader shares a vision. Share a vision of how you desire the process to work. Communicate how you expect and appreciate feedback for the betterment of the organization.

PRE-ROLLOUT DETERMINATIONS:

1. *Leadership team involvement—It is important to have the leadership team defined so that they will be notified on their involvement. The team can and should assist in cheerleading the process and accounting for their team's participation.*

2. *If you are an organization where you are the only person, or with a small staff, designate other business leaders whose opinions you value. Ask them to participate. Educate them on the process.*

3. *Define group meetings that will be necessary. This is determined by the size of an organization and how many locations, if more than one. Technology has allowed for internet connected meetings to be*

scheduled, however, in person meetings, when possible, still add value to demonstrate the importance of the program.

4. *Define how you will communicate. Things to be considered are:*

   A) *Spokesman—Usually top leader, however, this can be delegated.*

   B) *Email template communication announcing the program.*

   C) *Email template communication announcing the meeting and the process.*

   D) *Survey process: Paper or through Electronic Survey Process (Survey Monkey)*

   E) *How timeline, deadlines, and past due notifications will be communicated.*

   F) *How initial rollout meeting will be conducted.*

   G) *How the building of the Vision Statement will be conducted and communicated.*

   H) *How meeting for rollout of the Vision Statement will be conducted.*

   I) *Timeline for the process.*

PRE-ROLLOUT LEADERSHIP INITIAL MEETING:

1. Email Leadership Team of Meeting to define the organizations Vision Statement.

2. Send attached document explaining what a Vision Statement is. (Sample Enclosed)

3. If this is a re-assessment of an existing Vision Statement for the organization, then have each member bring a copy of current Vision Statement along with the milestones. Ask them to be prepared to give their assessment if the current Vision Statement is not being executed, or is achievable. Have leadership define if the current Vision needs to be changed, altered or re-purposed for another rollout.

4. Encourage each member to look at other organizations Vision Statement. Challenge them to define how that organization lives and demonstrates their Vision, and what they like or dislike about those examples.

5. Encourage openness and honesty, and respectfulness of others.

INITIAL MEETING—LEADERSHIP:
(CONDUCT ON BACK END OF MISSION STATEMENT INITIAL MEETING)

1. Have whiteboard ready or large wall-sized Post It Notes for hanging on wall.

2. If you have a current Vision Statement and if this is a re-assessment, then have a list with the current Vision Statement listed. Include milestones from the current Vision Statement.

3. Have each leader list considerations for a Vision, or their perception of the organizations current achievements, and what could or should be lofty goals. List these on whiteboard or large wall-sized Post It Notes.

4. Have each leader list a BHAG, Big Hairy Audacious Goal for their department, and for the whole organization.

5. Have each member explain why they believe they could accomplish their BHAG. Listen for the passion. Then ask the same question on the BHAG they listed for the whole organization. Listen to other comments in regards to other departments, debate and take notes.

5. Allow for respectful debate.

6. Define some good examples of a vision that can be developed into a Vison Statement for the organization. There does not have to be total agreement as the next stage of the process will debate, might eliminate, or add more.

INITIAL EMPLOYEE MEETING:
(SAME MEETING AS EMPLOYEE MISSION STATEMENT)

1. There is not a Vision Statement survey sent to employees in this process. Leadership executes the Mission Statement survey documented on exercise #2, completing their follow-up leadership meeting and defines the organizations Mission Statement. It is with the completion of the Mission Statement in the leadership follow-up meeting in exercise 2, that the leadership team then defines the organizations Vision Statement.

2. Explain to employee staff everything noted for the Mission Statement meeting. Then educate the staff on what a Vision Statement is, and explain that with the pending rollout of the Mission Statement, that the leadership team has been tasked with the development of a Vision Statement.

3. Explain the difference between a Mission Statement and a Vision Statement as one is external-facing and the other is internal-facing. Explain how one pulls the organization forward while the other pushes, and that both add value.

FOLLOW-UP LEADERSHIP MEETING:
(CONDUCTED ON THE BACK END OF FOLLOW-UP MISSION STATEMENT MEETING)

1. Have notes available from initial meeting, and have on display if possible.

2. Complete the leadership follow-up steps in exercise #2 in the development of a Mission Statement. Accept and adopt Mission Statement.

3. Ask the leadership team if there is any additional insight from the prior meeting in regards to vision.

4. Explain how the Vision needs to be aligned with the Mission. How the Mission Statement pulls the organization in a set direction with the Vision pushing, but the alignment has them heading in the same direction.

5. Re-explain a BHAG, Big Hairy Audacious Goal, 3 to 5 years out. (Samples Available)

6. Debate and define if the Vision should be 3 or 5 years out. Encourage 5 years with a 3 year evaluation. Decide and document.

7. Have each leader list BHAG's on whiteboard or large Post It Notes wall hangers.

8. Gain clarity as they are listed, eliminate duplicates or combine similar BHAG's.

9. Challenge for high expectations if necessary.

10. Seek if there are BHAG's that relate to:

    A) Growth

    B) New Products or Services

    C) Innovation

    D) Market Domination

    E) Community Impact

11. Debate each, do any of the BHAG's relate to each other?

12. Draft a few different Vision Statements, mix BHAG's together. Test combinations.

13. Debate and narrow down to two Vision Statements.

14. Debate if they are lofty, challenging, and a stretch. Correct if necessary.

15. Decide through debate and selection. Adopt a Vision Statement.

Important: Leadership is a molder of consensus not a builder of consensus. This means that the final determinations are made by the leader and the leadership team. The purpose of the exercise is to demonstrate openly and effectively that the process is inclusive, feedback is appreciated, and all things were taken into account.

16. Educate leadership on milestones, create and document milestones for the Vision Statements. (Milestones are predetermined measurements of progress with set timelines of expectations. When measured, it determines if progress on the Vision is being made, with an assessment of how much progress.)

17. Review with leadership team and ask openly:

    A) Does the Vision Statement challenge your organization to achieve with a lofty goal?

    B) Will the Vision Statement add clarity and help establish a strong culture?

    C) Does the Vision Statement represent how your organization should be driven by your internal customers, your employees?

    D) Does the Vision Statement include accountability?

    E) Can you live, stand, and not stray from the Vision Statement, even through difficult times?

    F) Does the Vision Statement allow for an evolving and changing industry while encouraging and supporting innovation?

    G) Can you envision the team rallying around the Vision Statement?

    E) Can you easily explain the benefits of the Vision Statement?

    F) Can you easily explain the milestones of the Vision Statement?

18. Final review, then adopt the Vision Statement.

19. Define how you want the Vision Statement listed. Remember, a Vision Statement is internal, so it should be in employee areas.

20. Define a communication plan. A communication plan includes:

    A) Timeline of dates and times of communications.

    B) How it will be communicated. (Live meeting, online meeting, etc.)

    C) Who will be presenting.

    D) Any marketing flyers for internal use. (Highly recommended)

    E) Materials that add to the marketing role out. (Balloons, food, drinks)

F) Website presence and recommendation on how to address it with customers.

G) Contest for demonstrating the Vision Statement.

H) Contest for memorizing the Vision Statement and benefits.

I) Expectations and accountability.

COMPANY ROLLOUT OF VISION STATEMENT MEETING:

This is the same meeting as the Mission Statement rollout meeting. Conduct all points of the Mission State-ment meeting and then address the Vision Statement as follows:

1. Be prepared to make it an exciting event. Be upbeat and add some fun and humor into the pre-sentation.

2. Give a quick review on the definition of a Vision Statement, how it is supposed to be challenging, with a 5 year vision.

3. Explain what a BHAG is, Big Hairy Audacious Goal, and why having BHAG's in a vision sets high expectations and pushes the team to achieve.

4. Explain the relationship between the Mission Statement and the Vision Statement. How both give guidance and the same direction. One pulls, which is the Mission Statement, and the other pushes, which is the Vision Statement.

5. Explain the expectations of everyone learning the Vision Statement and benefits through memo-rization, as well as holding each other accountable.

6. Pass out the marketing flyer on the Vision Statement and review. Explain each milestone and the importance in their measurement and achievement. Give real world examples that employees can relate to and understand.

7. Describe the contest recognizing employees who demonstrate through action that they are living the Vision Statement. Describe the rewards available, and timelines.

8. Review the expectation and importance of living the Vision Statement.

FOLLOWING DAYS AND WEEKS:

The most effective ways to follow-up is for you, as the leaders, to demonstrate the Vision Statement and its importance. Any meetings, whether live, over the phone, or through the internet, open each meeting by randomly quizzing individuals on the Vision Statement. Ask for examples of employees living the Vision Statement. Be fun, but also hold individuals accountable. Encourage individual employees that struggle, to learn the Vision Statement while expressing the importance. Your consistency on this process is what will demonstrate to others the importance. Your example will encourage other leaders to do the same, and eventually it will spread throughout the business.

Make sure any contest associated with the Vision Statement is followed up on and that all timelines are met. It is important to ensure that the Vision Statement gets integrated into the culture of the organization. Missing deadlines for contests is a killer of culture. When contest winners make achievements, reward results, and announce the achievement with communication. This communication can be live during a meeting, via email, announced on internal website, and intranet sites, etc. Make the prizes unique and even add in a twist, such as a unique business card for the winners. Be creative.

EVALUATION AND ASSESSMENT:

Vision Statements by definition should be 5 years out, but a 3 year evaluation is recommended. If leadership has been reviewing the milestones, an awareness of progress should be known. This is why it is recommended that an organization review their milestone progress and Vision Statement at the 3rd year mark. The assessment should appraise the current market environment, industry changes and challenges, and new innovation. An organization, at times, can out-pace their Vision and exceed expectations. If their Vision Statement has not changed, their employees can lose drive and initiative. If the Vision appears out of reach and it has been noticeable to employees, this can also cause lack of motivation. Technology changes industry faster each year, so evaluation is important.

EMAIL TEMPLATES—MISSION & VISION

Announcing the decision and process for building the organizations Mission Statement:

Subject: Our Mission Statement

To all employees,

All, we as an organization have decided and defined a process in which we will create and define our organizations Mission Statement. Because each of you are a valued part of our business, we need your participation, insight and feedback, so that we can construct a Mission Statement that we all believe and live each day, and that will demonstrate who we are as an organization. Our Mission Statement will help define our purpose as an organization and the reason for existence that we can display and execute for our external customers. The importance of defining our Mission Statement that matches our organizations values and principles is important as they will give us a set direction in achievement. Our values and principles will guide us daily. Our Mission Statement will lead us and our Vision Statement will push us all in the same direction. Great companies build and live their Mission, Vision and Values. Our values will build the foundation of every decision we make as an organization, starting with the Mission and Vision that then builds our strategic plans, initiatives, accountability plans, roadmaps, development plans, job descriptions, employee hiring and more. Let's make the process fun and exciting. You will be asked to participate in surveys and give feedback. Your response and timeliness will be greatly appreciated.

Meeting: (Announce place, time, and method of meeting)

Sincerely,

Management

Email announcing the Mission Statement Survey

Subject: Mission Statement Survey

To all employees,

As we move forward with the process of defining and adopting our organizations Mission Statement, please take a moment and answer the questions on the attached survey. There is an additional section for further comments and feedback. Your information will remain confidential. Timeliness is very important, and we desire and would like to achieve 100% participation. If you have any questions, please contact your supervisor or HR. (If survey is online simply supply the link or directions and adjust email)

Deadline: (Insert date)

Sincerely,

Management

Announcing the rollout of the Mission Statement.

Subject: Mission Statement Rollout Meeting!

To all employees,

It is with great excitement that we announce we have achieved our goal on building our organizations Mission Statement. Our Mission Statement will be the very definition on our purpose and reason for existence as an organization. The Mission, built on the foundation of our values and principles, serves as the foundation of every decision that our organization makes. We desire 100% participation to this important rollout meeting. We ask for your promptness and awareness.

Meeting date: (List date, time, duration and method of meeting.)

Sincerely,

Management

Email announcing importance of memorizing the Mission and Vision Statements

Subject: Importance of knowing our Mission and Vision Statements

To all employees,

Our organization has completed an important task in defining our Mission and Vision Statements. Your participation providing feedback and insight added invaluable contributions in their completion. With their completion, we as an organization must hold ourselves accountable by living and demonstrating them each day. Our marketing will display our Mission to our customers in our materials and website presence as well as provide visibility to the Vision through internal marketing. I implore each of us to commit them to our memory and celebrate them in action. We will have continual contests, rewards, and accountability to enhance our learning.

Sincerely,

Management

Email, sent at random times, announcing someone who has demonstrated the Mission.

Subject: Awesome display of our Mission (alter as needed)

To all employees,

I am so excited to see our Mission being demonstrated. *First Name Last Name* demonstrated our Mission by recognizing an area where we, as an organization, could assist a client achieve a larger goal within their own industry. *First Name Last Name* took initiative to understand the client's true objective in their industry and developed a solution that not only solves their problem, but the solution gives them a competitive edge and strategic advantage in their industry. This truly demonstrates to our customer our Mission Statement of, "Understanding our clients as if our life depended on it to help them achieve beyond their own expectations."

This is truly living our Mission Statement in action and I wanted to share with our entire staff. My personal thanks, *First Name Last Name*.

Sincerely,

Management

Email, sent at random times, announcing someone who has demonstrated the Vision.

Subject: Awesome display of our Vision (alter as needed)

To all employees,

I am so excited to see our Vision being demonstrated. *First Name Last Name* demonstrated our Vision by recognizing an area where we could utilize innovation, to build a new product line, stay ahead of our competition and lead our industry. This is outstanding! Remember our Vision Statement is, "To be innovative and continue to lead our industry with two product releases per year, while achieving 15% annual growth."

This is truly living our Vision Statement in action and I wanted to share with our entire staff. My personal thanks, *First Name Last Name.*

Sincerely,

Management

SURVEY—MISSION STATEMENT

Please answer the questions on this survey. Use all the space necessary as your feedback is greatly appreciated. Please be professional, yet forthright. Your comments and answers will be confidential.

1. What is the current Mission of our organization, if any? Do we demonstrate this Mission to our customers?

_____

_____

_____

_____

_____

2. Through an example, define our organizations purpose or reason for existence that we demonstrate to our customers?

_____

_____

_____

_____

3. Do you believe our organization is well educated on what our reason for existence is, and how to execute that daily?

_____

_____

_____

_____

_____

_____

4. If you were asked to list some ideas on what you believe our purpose as an organization would be, what would you list? Name at least three:

_____

_____

_____

_____

_____

_____

5. Why is a Mission Statement important in an organization in regards to their internal customers, the employees?

_____

_____

_____

_____

_____

6. Why is a Mission Statement important in an organization in regards to their external customers?

_____

_____

_____

_____

_____

_____

7. What companies, other than ours, do you believe effectively demonstrate their Mission Statement and why?

_____

_____

_____

_____

_____

_____

8. What are some of the best examples that other organizations use to display and exhibit their Mission Statement?

_____

_____

_____

_____

_____

9. Please rank the following on a scale of 1 through 10

       A) Educate Teams _____

       B) Empower Individuals _____

       C) Expand Knowledge _____

       D) Great Service _____

       E) Develop Partnerships _____

       F) Expand Innovation _____

       G) Develop New Technology _____

       H) Change Industry _____

       I) Market Leader _____

       J) Thought Leadership _____

10. Please provide your perception on the contribution and impact that this organization makes to the business community or should make?

_____

_____

_____

_____

Please provide any additional feedback.

_____

_____

_____

_____

_____

_____

Made in the USA
Middletown, DE
30 March 2019